The Zen CHRISTafarian Way

I0167030

By Andrew James Lutze

The Zen Christafarian Way

FIRST EDITION

———————————

Library of Congress Control Number: 2024 906114

———————————

ISBN 979-8-218-40400-0

To my mother

Margaret Lutze
and to my wife, Di Wu –
both of whom have nurtured my quirky curiosity and love of
freedom and independence

and to Peter J Lutze
my lion of a brother

and to Michael P. Nelson
a best friend like no other

With special appreciation to Rev. Edward Joseph Tomasiewicz,
Charles R. Strain, Ph.D., Elizabeth-Anne Stewart, Ph.D., and
Fr. James Halstead of the DePaul University Religious Studies
department for their shared wisdom given ever so generously

In loving memory of my grandfather Rev. Karl E. Lutze and my
grandmother Esther Lutze

and G. Paul Lenakos

Table of Contents

Preface

In the cacophony of modern life, where moral compasses seem to spin wildly and societal norms fluctuate with alarming frequency, the need for a guiding set of principles has never been more pressing. As I embarked on the journey of writing this book, I found myself deeply troubled by the moral decay and divisiveness permeating our society. It became apparent that amidst the chaos, we are in dire need of a spiritual compass to navigate the turbulent waters of contemporary existence.

The inspiration behind this book arose from a profound sense of dissatisfaction with the current state of affairs within Christianity. While once a steadfast beacon of moral guidance and spiritual enlightenment, Christianity seems to have lost its grip on the collective consciousness of society. In an age where amoral ideologies masquerade as progressive thought and Christian values are often sidelined or scorned, the urgency of reclaiming and revitalizing the essence of Christianity has become abundantly clear.

It is evident that traditional approaches to Christianity have faltered in the face of modern challenges. Christian leaders, often lacking in conviction and courage, seem to offer little resistance to the tide of moral relativism sweeping across the cultural landscape. In the midst of this crisis of faith, I was compelled to explore alternative paths that could breathe new life into the Christian tradition while remaining faithful to its core tenets.

After extensive immersion in the study of world religions and spiritual philosophies, I found myself drawn to two distinct traditions that offered profound insights and wisdom: Rastafarianism and Zen Buddhism. Though seemingly disparate in their origins and practices, both traditions share a common thread of seeking spiritual enlightenment and embodying principles of compassion, mindfulness, and ethical living.

The fusion of Christianity with Rastafarianism and Zen Buddhism represents a bold attempt to synthesize the wisdom of these diverse traditions into a cohesive framework that speaks to the needs of contemporary seekers. By borrowing insights from Rastafarianism's emphasis on harmonious community-minded living, righteous justice, and reverence for nature, as well as Zen Buddhism's focus on mindfulness, non-attachment, and self-awareness, I seek to offer a holistic approach to Christianity that is both relevant and transformative.

The aim of this book is to not dilute or distort the essence of Christianity, but rather to enrich and expand its horizons by integrating the wisdom of other spiritual traditions. It is an attempt to take a fresh look at Christianity and how it can be strengthened through multiple lenses and perspectives. By embracing diversity and fostering dialogue between different faiths, we have the opportunity to uncover deeper truths and insights that transcend the limitations of any single tradition. This, in turn, will hopefully lead people who would otherwise see Christianity as something more archaic and outdated to view it as something relevant and practical in our modern age.

At its core, this book is an invitation to embark on a journey of spiritual exploration and discovery—a journey that transcends dogma and doctrine in search of a deeper, more authentic experience of faith. It is my hope that through the insights and practices shared within these pages, readers will find inspiration, guidance, and renewed purpose in their own spiritual journeys.

As we navigate the complexities of the modern world, let us not lose sight of the timeless wisdom that has guided seekers for millennia. Let us reclaim the power of faith to transform hearts and minds, and to heal the wounds of a fractured world. Together, let us embark on a journey towards a more enlightened and courageous expression of Christianity—one that honors its rich tradition while embracing the ever-evolving tapestry of human spirituality.

Introduction

Human nature intrinsically seeks out a moral and philosophical compass. Children are filled with a natural curiosity to constantly seek answers and understanding. Similarly, throughout life, the healthy adult will consistently reflect on moral issues as complex situations arise. Life is full of challenges, and there is not always a clear black and white solution. Coupled with this is the fact that perspectives can shift and change according to point of view, context, and along with the various filters we may shift through within our experiences of a shared reality. Without a strong set of ideals, values, and guiding principles, humanity is set adrift aimlessly wandering in darkness and bound to create even more suffering than that which already is prescribed by the physical trials that are an unavoidable part of life in the human form. Luckily for us, we do not have to start from scratch in order to find a way to make the most of life and find a way to move through it with mindful awareness, joy, compassion, and enduring strength.

Religion as Identity

The word "religion" impacts individuals in many different ways and carries all sorts of connotations. For many, it can be a very strict way of life that recognizes a specific deity or set of deities to be worshipped in specific ways. It can be very exclusive in the sense that those who adhere to a particular religion may see others who do not subscribe to that same group identity as "other" or a threat or just lost perhaps. In that way, religion can be seen as belonging to a certain club or tribe which can be comforting for those who have a strong need for a sense of belonging and community. It serves as a defining aspect of one's identity, setting them apart from those who adhere to different beliefs. This sense of belonging is deeply cherished, sometimes to the extent that straying from the established norms carries significant repercussions. This may include the more extremely faithful who see religious faith as a life-or-death decision, which includes the potential destruction or enslavement of the soul in the realm of the eternal. For these religious devotees, ritual and dogmatic rigidity are often uncompromising and add to the more exclusive characteristics that can coincide with a particular religion's identity or sect.

The "Unreligous" View

For others, religion is a very unappealing and even offensive term. Many atheists see religion as a relatively negative flaw of humanity. Intellectuals and materialists who reject religion will point to a lack of empirical scientific evidence for most religious claims. It can sometimes be described as a projection of archetypal human traits in extreme form and attributed to some mystical supernatural or even allegorical entity. They see religion as an antiquated way that ancient people used to try to make sense out of things that were beyond human comprehension. Often, those who reject religion will take the view that people currently are religious for the sake of tradition or due to simple naivety. For materialist atheists, Science has replaced religion as the structure with which to make sense of the world including inexplicable phenomena.

A Broader View of Religion

A third or alternate way to view religion would be more of an anthropological or cultural approach. This could include some appreciation for mystical beliefs, doctrines, canons, and faith-based practices. However, here the focus concentrates more on lifestyles, philosophical understandings, implementation of specific teachings, social impact, ethical behavior, and general wisdom. This approach allows us to expand beyond the confines of religious dogma and borrow from the wellspring of understandings gained by the steadfast diligence and discoveries of those who devoted their lives to making sense of the world and dedicated themselves to making it a better place as well as making it easier to navigate through this journey called life.

The Quest for Connection and Meaning

Humanity's pursuit of spirituality transcends cultures, eras, and individual beliefs, etched into the fabric of our existence. At its core lies an innate yearning for understanding, connection, and meaning beyond the tangible realms. Both common sense and intuition tell us that there is an elegant intelligence that harmonizes what otherwise would be a chaotic universe. The ideas of natural laws, mathematics, physics, and a unified theory are all completely dependent on the notion of something much greater and more conscious than what we can perceive with our limited and veiled awareness. Throughout history, this quest has manifested in diverse forms, from organized religions to personal philosophies, reflecting humanity's collective longing for transcendence and purpose.

Spanning civilizations, spirituality has served as a compass guiding individuals through the maze of existence. It addresses our existential questions, offering solace amidst uncertainty and instilling a sense of belonging to something greater. At the same time, it affirms our own place in the universe and compels us to play an active role in the expression of creation. Whether through prayer, meditation, rituals, or contemplation, the human spirit seeks communion with the divine, striving for a deeper comprehension of life's mysteries.

Interestingly, spirituality extends its embrace beyond the confines of religion, resonating with even those who identify as atheists or agnostics. It represents an innate human impulse for transcendence, urging us to explore realms beyond the mundane and uncover layers of meaning that enrich our experiences. For the uninitiated, this can be expressed through the appreciation of art, music, poetry, dance, and other forms that have added meaning beyond the pragmatic needs of survival. This universal quest underscores the interconnectedness of all beings, emphasizing the shared human desire for a sense of significance and connectedness to the universe.

The pursuit of spirituality often acts as a unifying force, fostering empathy and understanding among diverse communities. It transcends cultural divides, emphasizing common values of compassion, kindness, and a reverence for life. It serves as a catalyst for empathy, encouraging individuals to seek understanding beyond differences and embrace the inherent humanity in others. Spirituality also humbles the ego as it elevates the divine above the aspirations of the individual and above the desire for personal gain.

How Everyone Benefits

In essence, humanity's quest for spirituality encapsulates the perennial search for purpose, transcendence, and interconnectedness. It is an enduring journey that navigates the complexities of existence, offering a path towards inner peace, communal harmony, and a deeper comprehension of our place in the vast orchestra of the cosmos. It is an acknowledgement on a deep personal level of the idea of an infinite and intelligent creation interacting with itself.

Atheists and agnostics, while not subscribing to specific religious doctrines, can glean profound insights and invaluable wisdom from exploring diverse religious perspectives. Engaging with various religious teachings and practices offers a rich mosaic of ethical, moral, and philosophical insights that transcend the boundaries of faith. These perspectives serve as reservoirs of accumulated human wisdom, presenting different lenses through which to view the world, grapple with existential questions, and navigate life's complexities. By embracing the diverse tapestry of religions, atheists and agnostics can tap into these deep reservoirs of human experience, finding guidance on ethical dilemmas, moral principles, and existential contemplations. These perspectives can foster a broader understanding of cultural heritage, promoting empathy, tolerance, and an appreciation for diverse worldviews. Religion, in its essence, offers a repository of narratives, rituals, and moral frameworks that can enrich lives by providing a sense of community, offering guidance in navigating personal struggles, and imparting a moral compass to guide one's actions. Thus, atheists and agnostics, by exploring religious perspectives, can find value in the profound wisdom distilled from centuries of human introspection, enabling a more nuanced and enriched understanding of the human experience.

For my fellow Christians who may feel they need to strictly adhere only to Biblical teachings and that they must reject all other perspectives as either "wrong", "blasphemy" or even "evil", I ask you to consider the following. The richness of our faith lies not only in the pages of the Bible but also in the diversity of spiritual perspectives that grace our world. As believers, we are called to embrace the wisdom and truths that resonate with the essence of our Christian faith, recognizing that spiritual enlightenment can often come from unexpected sources. Scripture itself attests to the broader understanding that truth is not confined to a single source. In Proverbs 11:14, it is written, "Where there is no guidance, a people falls, but in an abundance of counselors, there is safety." This wisdom encourages us to seek knowledge and wisdom from various sources. Our faith journey is not limited to a solitary path but is enriched by the intersection of various spiritual perspectives. Many facets of Christianity, including its rituals and traditions, draw from diverse origins beyond the Bible, such as elements from Judaism and other spiritual traditions. If we close ourselves off from other teachings solely because they do not derive from the Bible, we risk denying ourselves the wealth of knowledge and experiences that life has to offer. Moreover, this exclusionary stance can lead to incongruent and hypocritical situations, as our faith is not about shutting out differing beliefs but about discerning and embracing truths that resonate with the essence of our Christian values. After all, why was Jesus rejected by most of his fellow Jews during his lifetime? Simply put, he was unexpected. They were so rooted and entrenched in their dogma and so confined in a particular worldview that they simply were not ready to be open to the new perspectives being brought forth by Jesus. Embracing a broader spectrum of spiritual perspectives does not weaken our faith; instead, it fortifies our understanding, enriches our spiritual journey, and brings us closer to the profound truths embedded within the Bible.

Just as each experience in life, whether abundantly joyful or intensely traumatic (or anywhere in between), can provide us with a lesson and lasting wisdom, so too can each religion or philosophy help us to fill in the gaps when it comes to broadening our perspectives and creating the version of reality we wish to experience. As we find ourselves in a world moving forward at an unprecedented pace in terms of technology, information, communication, and social change, it can be a dizzying process filled with confusion unless we find a way to anchor ourselves in something more timeless such that we find in the ideas and principles common to many religions. With moral relativism, dissolution of traditional families, social problems, income disparity, and societal division in general on the increase, many are seeking a new way forward that can address humanity's need for moral guidance, understanding, unity, and most of all - love.

This book takes three great religious/philosophical approaches and attempts to begin to synthesize them in a harmonious synergy that can appeal to all seekers of wisdom and guidance. These three religions were not just chosen at random. There are very specific value-adds that each approach has to offer, and they are compatible in a way that brings forth a profound and unique worldview. The Zen Christafarian way has at its center (both figuratively and literally) "Christ". One would not err to call this a Christian perspective. However, this Christian perspective takes what would be called a "Zen" approach to Christianity rooted in pure awareness, meditation, and aligning with the natural order of things also known as the Dao/Tao or "the Way". The other supporting structure to this new Christian perspective includes elements of Rastafarian culture as implied by the suffix added onto the word "Christ". As will be discussed in the corresponding section, Rastafari as a movement is already an offshoot of Christianity, and this book will show appreciation for the cultural bounty provided by the Rastas. By the end, our synthesis will illustrate a balance between self-awareness, humility and love of your fellow humans through Christ, and how to live a natural life of courage.

CHAPTER 1

The development of Zen Buddhism

The Development of Zen Buddhism

Zen Buddhism, often regarded as an enigmatic yet profound school of Buddhism, finds its roots in the ancient teachings of Siddhartha Gautama, the historical Buddha. Its emergence can be traced back to India, where Buddhism itself originated around the 6th century BCE. The development of Zen, known as Chan (禅) in China before it reached Japan, is a testament to the adaptability and transformative nature of Buddhist thought across cultures and epochs.

The inception of Zen can be linked to the teachings of Mahayana Buddhism, emphasizing the pursuit of enlightenment and the awakening of all sentient beings. However, it was in China during the 6th century CE that Zen began to take shape as a distinct school of Buddhist thought. Bodhidharma, a legendary figure, is often credited as the first patriarch of Zen Buddhism. He is said to have traveled from India to China and transmitted the lineage of what would later become Zen teachings at the Shaolin Temple. Bodhidharma's emphasis on meditation, self-realization, and the direct transmission of enlightenment laid the groundwork for Zen's future development.

Throughout its evolution in China, Zen was greatly influenced by the integration of Buddhist principles with Chinese Daoist philosophy and Confucianism. In fact, many Chinese viewed Buddhism as a foreign version of Daoism, so it was quite easily adopted and the fusion was a natural process. Notable figures like Huineng, the sixth patriarch of Chan Buddhism, played pivotal roles in shaping Zen's direction. Huineng's teachings emphasized the idea of sudden enlightenment, a concept that became central to Zen practice. His Platform Sutra, a foundational text, elucidated the nature of enlightenment as inherent in everyone and attainable through direct experience rather than extensive study or ritual. This was a rather revolutionary idea at the time.

However, it was during the Tang Dynasty (618–907 CE) that Zen flourished, with the establishment of various Zen schools and the development of unique practices. The emphasis on meditation, known as zazen, became integral to Zen training. The renowned teacher Mazu Daoyi, along with his successors, introduced the use of koans—paradoxical statements or questions—to provoke enlightenment experiences beyond conceptual understanding.

The transition of Zen to Japan occurred primarily through the efforts of Dogen Zenji, a Japanese monk who traveled to China to study Zen in the 13th century. On his return, he founded the Soto Zen school, emphasizing the practice of zazen as the essence of enlightenment itself. Concurrently, another influential figure, Eisai, introduced Rinzai Zen in Japan, emphasizing koan study and the importance of sudden awakening experiences.

The subsequent development of Zen in Japan witnessed the emergence of notable figures such as Hakuin Ekaku, who revitalized Rinzai Zen and promoted the use of koans as a means of reaching enlightenment. Hakuin's writings and teachings revitalized the practice and provided guidance for generations of Zen practitioners.

Zen Buddhism's core principles revolve around direct experiential realization, emphasizing the innate potential of every individual to awaken to their true nature. It encourages a direct, non-conceptual understanding of reality, transcending language and doctrine. Zazen, koan study, and the guidance of a teacher (roshi) are pivotal in Zen practice, emphasizing the immediacy of enlightenment, which is accessible in the present moment rather than a distant future.

The evolution of Zen Buddhism mirrors its continual adaptation and refinement, blending philosophical insights with practical methodologies aimed at awakening. From its origins in India to its growth in China and eventual transmission to Japan, Zen has embraced various cultural contexts while preserving its core emphasis on direct experience, meditation, and the pursuit of enlightenment. Its enduring legacy lies in its ability to offer a transformative path to realization, resonating across diverse cultures and eras as a profound means of awakening to the fundamental nature of existence.

CHAPTER 2

What is unique about Zen Buddhism?

What is Unique about Zen Buddhism?

Zen Buddhism stands in stark contrast to dogmatic religions in its fundamental approach to spirituality, placing a distinct emphasis on experiential learning and eschewing conventional religious structures. Unlike many dogmatic religions that emphasize adherence to rigid doctrines, prescribed beliefs, and elaborate rituals, Zen Buddhism is characterized by its direct, experiential approach to understanding reality and achieving enlightenment. It requires that one is fully present in the moment whereas our habit is to be otherwise preoccupied with past events and/or future planning – the understanding being that both past and future can only exist in this now moment.

Dogmatic religions often rely on established texts, doctrines, and hierarchical structures that dictate beliefs and practices. In contrast, Zen Buddhism places greater significance on personal experience and direct realization over scriptural authority or dogma. Rather than relying solely on scriptures or theological tenets, Zen encourages practitioners to engage in meditation (zazen) and direct introspection, seeking enlightenment through personal experience rather than blind adherence to established beliefs. Each one of us is a unique expression in this interconnected existence and therefore must uniquely and individually find our own moment(s) of enlightenment.

In particular, dogmatic religions tend to emphasize the attainment of salvation or a predetermined goal set by religious authorities. Zen, however, focuses on the present moment and the immediate experience of reality. It advocates for mindfulness and being fully present in each moment, highlighting the importance of realizing enlightenment here and now rather than in some distant future or afterlife. The Zen perspective is constantly beckoning us to cease drifting into imagination, recollection, projection and nostalgia – it yanks us right back into the newness of this very moment.

Traditional religious structures often involve complex hierarchies, clergy, and ceremonial practices. Zen Buddhism, on the other hand, minimizes these structures, emphasizing direct teacher-student transmission and a more informal setting for spiritual guidance. The role of a Zen master (roshi) is not to act as an intermediary between the practitioner and the divine but rather as a guide facilitating the practitioner's own realization through direct experience.

In contrast to dogmatic religions that may emphasize belief in a particular deity or pantheon of gods, Zen Buddhism is non-theistic in nature. While it does not deny the existence of deities, it focuses on personal experience and the inherent Buddha nature that is within each individual. This departure from theism enables practitioners to delve deeper into understanding the nature of self and reality without being bound by theological dogmas.

Dogmatic religions often cultivate a sense of separateness between the sacred and the mundane, prescribing specific rituals or spaces as holier or more spiritually significant. In Zen, there is an emphasis on the integration of spiritual practice into everyday life. The distinction between the sacred and profane dissolves, and simple acts like eating, walking, or working become opportunities for mindful practice and realization. This implicates the omnipresence of the divine.

While dogmatic religions may have established moral codes or commandments, Zen Buddhism emphasizes moral conduct rooted in compassion and wisdom derived from direct insight into reality. The ethical principles of Zen arise naturally from the practitioner's deepened understanding rather than from external rules or authorities.

Moreover, dogmatic religions often offer clear-cut answers to metaphysical questions about the afterlife, providing believers with a sense of certainty. In contrast, Zen challenges practitioners to embrace uncertainty and transcend dualistic thinking. It encourages the exploration of paradoxes and the experience of ambiguity, aiming for a direct realization of truth beyond conceptual understanding.

Another significant departure from dogmatic religions lies in the use of koans in Zen practice. Koans are paradoxical statements or questions designed to provoke the practitioner into breaking free from logical reasoning and conceptual thinking, aiming at a direct, non-intellectual understanding of reality. This approach contrasts sharply with the systematic and often literal interpretations of religious scriptures found in dogmatic religions.

In summary, Zen Buddhism distinguishes itself from dogmatic religions by prioritizing direct experiential learning, eschewing rigid doctrinal structures, emphasizing present-moment realization, and inviting practitioners to transcend dualistic thinking through direct insight and practice. Its emphasis on personal experience, mindfulness, and direct realization marks a departure from the dogmas and conventional structures prevalent in many established religious traditions.

CHAPTER 3

The Zen Way

The Zen "Way"

D.T. Suzuki, Alan Watts, and Thich Nhat Hanh are pivotal figures who popularized Zen Buddhism in the West, elucidating its principles and demonstrating how they can be integrated into everyday life. These mavericks had revolutionary ways of presenting Zen concepts and were largely responsible for the spread of Zen into popular culture. They were in tune with the zeitgeist of their generations and had the ability to convey difficult concepts in a simple way that captivated those seeking to understand archetypal truths.

D.T. Suzuki, a Japanese scholar, played a crucial role in introducing Zen to the Western audience. He emphasized the experiential aspect of Zen, advocating for direct insight into reality. Suzuki's teachings revolved around the concept of "satori," a sudden awakening or enlightenment experience achievable through dedicated practice. His works, such as "Zen and Japanese Culture," delved into the intersection of Zen philosophy with art, aesthetics, and daily life. Suzuki highlighted the importance of mindfulness, asserting that one can experience the profundity of Zen in ordinary activities by being fully present in each moment. Practical integration of Zen, according to Suzuki, involved cultivating mindfulness in all actions, whether mundane or significant, by immersing oneself wholly in the present moment.

Alan Watts, a British-American philosopher, popularized Eastern philosophies, including Zen, in the West. He interpreted Zen principles in a way accessible to Western audiences, emphasizing the interconnectedness of all things. Watts advocated for the dissolution of the ego-bound self, urging individuals to transcend dualistic thinking and embrace the unity of existence. His teachings focused on the concept of "wu-wei," or effortless action, stressing the importance of spontaneity and non-striving. Watts encouraged individuals to relinquish the illusion of control and embrace life's flow. Integrating Zen into everyday life, as per Watts, involved letting go of the constant pursuit of goals and learning to simply "be," allowing life to unfold naturally without resistance.

Thich Nhat Hanh, a Vietnamese Zen master, emphasized mindfulness as a means of cultivating inner peace and social harmony. His teachings revolved around the practice of "mindfulness in everyday life," emphasizing the significance of being fully present in each moment. Nhat Hanh introduced the concept of "walking meditation," encouraging individuals to be aware of each step, cultivating mindfulness even in simple acts like walking. He advocated for engaged Buddhism, urging practitioners to apply mindfulness to address societal issues. Integrating Zen into daily life, according to Nhat Hanh, involved cultivating compassion and understanding in interactions, practicing deep listening, and nurturing mindfulness in every action, whether eating, working, or communicating.

The teachings of Suzuki, Watts, and Nhat Hanh converge on the practical integration of Zen principles into everyday life. They emphasize mindfulness as a key practice, urging individuals to be fully present in each moment, whether engaged in routine activities or facing challenges. The central idea revolves around cultivating awareness, relinquishing the incessant chatter of the mind, and embracing the richness of the present moment. We spend much of our time living unconsciously, often obsessing about the past, anticipating some future event, or engulfing our attention in some sort of distraction in hopes of feeling pleasure and excitement. Being mindful puts us in the driver's seat when it comes to conscious awareness. It is a way of taking full responsibility for one's involvement with creation and truly living with intention.

Their teachings highlight the transformative power of everyday experiences, inviting individuals to perceive the extraordinary within the ordinary. Integrating Zen into daily life involves a shift in perspective, transcending the mundane and discovering profound meaning in simple actions. It requires a commitment to mindfulness, a practice of being fully attentive and aware of thoughts, feelings, and sensations arising in each moment.

The integration of Zen principles involves embracing impermanence and letting go of attachments. It simply and bluntly acknowledges that earthly material things are fluid and just as a beautiful aroma wafting through the air may grab your attention and stimulate your taste buds, it is futile to attempt to capture or contain it. Zen calls for an understanding of the interconnectedness of all beings and events, fostering empathy, and compassionate engagement with the world. Our minds are very powerful tools. Just as one who wields a floor buffer or sanding belt must have training and steady discipline lest the tool spin or slide uncontrollably potentially causing great injury, we too must train our minds so that they serve us and do not harm us. In other words, mind your mind.

In essence, Suzuki, Watts, and Nhat Hanh emphasized the practical application of Zen principles in daily life, urging individuals to infuse mindfulness, compassion, and awareness into their everyday experiences, fostering a deeper sense of connection, peace, and fulfillment. Their teachings offer profound guidance on navigating an authentic and harmonious existence within a world rife with distractions and complexities.

They unravel the intricacies that often ensnare us, particularly in a society where the pursuit of material wealth complicates our lives, leading us to lose touch with our roots and the innate bond with nature.

Of course, no analysis of Zen practice can be complete without mentioning the work of Shunryu Suzuki. Shunryu Suzuki's influential book, "Zen Mind, Beginner's Mind," has become a cornerstone in the exploration of Zen philosophy, offering profound insights into the essence of living by the way of Zen. One key theme that permeates Suzuki's teachings is the concept of "naturalness." In emphasizing the importance of naturalness, Suzuki guides readers towards embracing an unadorned, unpretentious approach to life. The book encourages individuals to shed preconceived notions and societal conditioning, urging them to reconnect with the simplicity and authenticity of their true selves. As we will see later, these themes resonate deeply with both the original expressions of Christianity as well as Rastafarianism. Through cultivating naturalness, Suzuki asserts that one can attain a deeper understanding of the present moment, fostering a sense of mindfulness and tranquility.

Suzuki's exploration of "God-giving" is another significant aspect of "Zen Mind, Beginner's Mind." The concept challenges traditional dualistic thinking by proposing that the divine is not an external force to be sought but an intrinsic aspect of our being. By acknowledging the immanence of the divine within ourselves and our surroundings, Suzuki invites readers to transcend dualistic perceptions and recognize the interconnectedness of all things. This profound shift in perspective aligns with Zen principles, emphasizing the unity of the self with the universe.

"Zen Mind, Beginner's Mind" delves into the core of Zen philosophy, exploring the principle of "non-duality." Suzuki emphasizes the interconnectedness of all phenomena, breaking down the artificial barriers that separate self from other, subject from object. The book challenges the conventional dualistic view that pervades our understanding of the world, encouraging readers to recognize the interdependence and oneness inherent in all aspects of life. Through the lens of non-duality, Suzuki invites individuals to transcend divisive thinking and perceive the inherent unity that underlies all existence.

Ultimately, "Zen Mind, Beginner's Mind" offers a timeless guide for people from all walks of life to improve and enhance their well-being. Suzuki's teachings provide practical insights into navigating the complexities of modern existence with simplicity, mindfulness, and a profound awareness of the interconnectedness of all things. By embracing naturalness, recognizing the God-giving nature within, and understanding non-duality, individuals can cultivate a more harmonious and meaningful way of living. The book stands as an enduring source of wisdom, guiding readers toward a transformative journey that transcends cultural and religious boundaries, offering a universal path towards personal growth and enlightenment.

CHAPTER 4

The redemption song that is Christianity

The Redemption Song that is Christianity

The concept of redemption within Christianity stands as a cornerstone of its teachings, embodying the transformative power of forgiveness, grace, and salvation. At its core, redemption signifies the process of being saved or delivered from sin, spiritual bondage, and the consequences of human fallibility through the sacrificial act of Jesus Christ. This singular concept catapults Christianity to a transcendent realm, surpassing all other forms of religious expression. It not only recognizes the intrinsic limitations of our consciousness and the frailty within our human nature but, far from consigning us to perpetual victimhood for our mistakes and inherent flaws, infuses a profound sense of hope and strength. It propels the belief that persistent improvement in our perspectives and actions is possible, guiding us steadfastly onto the transformative path of righteousness.

Christianity proclaims that humanity, marred by sin and separated from God, finds restoration and reconciliation through Christ's redemptive act on the cross. The belief in Jesus as the savior who sacrificed himself for the salvation of humanity lies at the heart of Christian redemption. The narrative of redemption signifies the divine initiative of God's love and mercy, offering forgiveness and a pathway to spiritual renewal. Of note and monumental significance is that this applies even to the "lowest" individuals in society. Each and every single human being is welcomed into the arms of Christ.

Redemption within Christianity is not merely a theological doctrine but an experiential reality that impacts personal growth and spirituality. It provides a framework for understanding human imperfection and the possibility of transformation through faith. The transformative power of redemption is evident in the personal stories of individuals who have experienced spiritual rebirth and liberation from the burdens of guilt and sin.

Central to the Christian concept of redemption is the idea of atonement (at-ONE-ment with God), signifying the reconciliation between God and humanity through Jesus Christ. The sacrificial death of Christ is perceived as the ultimate expression of God's love and grace, offering humanity a chance at spiritual renewal and a restored relationship with the divine. It wipes the whole slate clean and we can begin anew once we decide to align our intentions with those of the Holy Spirit.

The transformative impact of redemption is profound, leading individuals to experience a sense of liberation, inner healing, and the renewal of the human spirit. It offers a path towards forgiveness, allowing individuals to release feelings of guilt, shame, and regret, and embrace a renewed sense of purpose and identity. Without this notion, many can become completely overwhelmed and the feelings so heavy that they may no longer choose life.

Redemption's transformative power extends beyond personal salvation; it permeates ethical and moral dimensions, inspiring believers to embody compassion, forgiveness, and altruism. It serves as a catalyst for personal growth, motivating individuals to strive for moral excellence and a life reflective of Christ's teachings. Once one feels their burdens lifted, it becomes a gift where they can display similar compassion towards others and make their lives a bit lighter in turn. Redemption serves as a source of hope and resilience in times of adversity and suffering. It provides solace and assurance that even amidst life's trials and tribulations, there exists a promise of spiritual restoration and eternal life.

Christian spirituality is deeply intertwined with the concept of redemption, inducing a profound relationship with God and a sense of belonging within the Christian community. It invites believers into a journey of spiritual growth, encouraging a deeper understanding of faith, grace, and the transformative love of God. It is giving the green light to let go of the need to control and make sense of every single thing in life and just let God guide – knowing all the time that things will turn out as they should in the end.

Redemption's impact on spirituality extends to communal aspects, fostering a sense of unity and fellowship among believers. It encourages individuals to extend grace and forgiveness towards others, promoting harmony and reconciliation within communities. Trust in God expands outward to your brothers and sisters on earth where bonds of trust can grow and thrive. The concept of redemption underscores the idea of second chances and new beginnings. It inspires individuals to embrace change, to seek reconciliation, and to embark on a journey of continuous spiritual growth and renewal.

In essence, the concept of redemption within Christianity embodies a transformative narrative of divine love, grace, and salvation. Its impact on personal growth and spirituality is profound, offering individuals a path towards forgiveness, spiritual renewal, moral transformation, and a deep-rooted sense of connection with God and fellow believers. The redemptive story of Christianity serves as a beacon of hope, guiding believers on a transformative journey toward spiritual wholeness and eternal life.

CHAPTER 5

Christian Ethics in Society

Christian Ethics in Society

In the absence of shared guiding principles and a universal moral compass, society becomes susceptible to misunderstanding, confusion, conflicts, and destructive actions perpetrated by both collective entities and individuals alike. Christian values play a significant role in shaping societal ethics and promoting a harmonious community by emphasizing moral principles that extend into societal and business contexts. Throughout history, numerous nations and communities have embraced a Christian identity, harnessing its principles to propel society towards harmony, freedom, unity, and compassion. However, amidst this trajectory, some contend that conflicts, atrocities, and the manifestation of evil have been perpetrated under the guise of Christ's guidance. It is an undeniable truth that malevolent individuals, propelled by deceit or calamitous events, can ascend to positions of power, perpetrating sin even within predominantly Christian societies. Volumes have been penned, delving into this subject's complexities. Yet, amidst these discussions, a potent and pivotal concept emerges, especially concerning governments rooted in Christian ethos: the notion of God-bestowed "inalienable" rights. These rights stand as immutable, beyond the purview of human bestowal or revocation—they are fundamental and inviolable. When a society comprehends these fundamental rights, as enshrined in documents like our

Declaration of Independence, it erects barriers curtailing the potential for despots seeking godlike authority to inflict atrocities upon the populace. It is only when those in positions of power disregard this fundamental principle that humanity bears the brunt of immense inhumanity.

At the core of Christian values lie the principles of love, compassion, and the inherent worth of every individual. These values promote the idea of treating others with dignity, respect, and empathy, creating a solid sense of community and interconnectedness. Love, as exemplified in the teachings of Jesus Christ, serves as a guiding principle for ethical conduct, urging individuals to prioritize the well-being of others above personal gain. After all, the most selfless thing to do is to treat others as if they are you, and even the selfish must eventually understand that one cannot serve thyself without others. In fact, by serving others, you are serving yourself. Knowing that this pleases God is service to All.

Christian values emphasize the importance of honesty, integrity, and ethical behavior in both societal and business realms. The teachings of Jesus Christ, advocating for truthfulness and transparency, underscore the significance of integrity in personal and professional interactions. This ethical framework encourages individuals to uphold honesty and fairness in dealings, fostering trust and reliability within communities and business environments. When faced with the decision of choosing contractors and business associates, a Christian perspective might incline one toward individuals or entities known for embodying a spirit of communal care and consideration, reflecting the values of looking out for the well-being of all rather than adopting a solely self-serving or competitive approach.

The concept of justice is another fundamental Christian value that influences societal harmony. Christianity advocates for social egalitarianism, urging individuals to stand against oppression, inequality, and exploitation. The pursuit of justice aligns with the Christian call to alleviate suffering and promote equality, contributing to the establishment of a more stable and cohesive society. Christians, no matter how compassionate or forgiving, should always speak out against injustice and promote those who seek just dealings. Turning the other cheek is not the same as turning a blind eye.

Christian values promote the importance of humility, forgiveness, and reconciliation. These principles promote a culture of understanding and compassion, encouraging individuals to seek forgiveness, extend grace, and reconcile differences. In societal contexts, the practice of forgiveness advances healing, reconciliation, and the restoration of relationships, contributing to overall social harmony and unity. Even in small towns, misunderstanding and miscarriages of justice are bound to occur. When there is a general attitude of forgiveness along with righting the wrongs that were done, those communities will flourish.

Christian values also advocate for stewardship and care for the environment. The belief in God as the creator of all things instills a sense of responsibility to protect and preserve the natural world. This perspective encourages sustainable practices and ethical considerations in business operations, promoting environmental conservation and responsible resource management. Just as Genesis entrusted humanity with the stewardship of the Earth, Christians, inspired by biblical teachings, embrace the sacred duty of environmental care, cultivating a profound connection between faith and ecological responsibility. All true Christians revere nature and healthy environmental conditions.

In the business realm, Christian values should influence ethical decision-making and practices. They promote a commitment to fair treatment of employees, customers, and stakeholders. Business ethics rooted in Christian principles prioritize ethical conduct, fair labor practices, and responsible stewardship of resources, contributing to a more transparent and ethical business environment. A boss can be both effective and moral in order for a company to thrive – any notion otherwise is a short-sighted goal rooted in manipulative practice.

Christian values emphasize the importance of service and altruism. The principle of serving others selflessly aligns with societal welfare and contributes to the establishment of a compassionate and supportive community. Within businesses, this value manifests in corporate social responsibility initiatives and philanthropic endeavors aimed at benefiting communities and addressing societal needs. This should not be viewed as mere obligation, but it should be seen as an honor as those who have the ability to do so can and should in order to contribute as a member of God's community. Just as the separate distinct components of your body may have diverging functions and abilities, they all serve a greater purpose.

Christian values provide a moral compass for individuals and institutions, guiding actions and decisions toward ethical conduct and social responsibility. They contribute to the establishment of a society that prioritizes compassion, justice, integrity, and mutual respect, fostering an environment conducive to harmonious coexistence and societal well-being. These values serve as a framework for ethical behavior, promoting a culture of respect, fairness, and care within both societal and business contexts.

CHAPTER 6

Christian mysticism and "The Way"

Christian Mysticism and "The Way"

Hans Urs von Balthasar, a prominent Swiss theologian, delved into the concept of God as "Love" in his work "Love Alone." His exploration of Christian mysticism centered around the notion of love as the defining attribute of God's nature, presenting a profound understanding of divine love and its implications for human spirituality. Hans is a Christian mystic, a "Natural Mystic", that went to the deepest core of understanding with regard to Christianity and God as Love.

Von Balthasar's concept of God as "Love" encapsulates the essence of Christian mysticism. He emphasizes that love is not merely an attribute of God but is inherent to God's very being. This divine love, according to von Balthasar, is self-giving, sacrificial, and unconditional—a love that seeks to draw humanity into a deeper communion with the divine. This profound love not only grants us the freedom to explore and occasionally lose our way but also provides the means to rediscover our path through the gift of free will. In our obscured existence and within the confines of our limited consciousness, it is the same boundless Love that defines God's essence. This Love, omnipresent and ever-pervading, resonates within us, acting as a magnetic force drawing us toward our authentic selves and, simultaneously, beckoning us toward His divine kingdom.

Drawing upon the mystical tradition, von Balthasar's concept resonates with the teachings of other Christian mystics, such as Meister Eckhart, Julian of Norwich, and Teresa of Ávila. Meister Eckhart was a medieval mystic, who spoke of the soul's union with God through an intimate and transformative experience of divine love. Similarly, Julian of Norwich's revelations centered on the unconditional love of God, portraying God as a nurturing and compassionate presence. Teresa of Ávila, in her mystical experiences, emphasized the ecstatic union with God, characterized by an overwhelming sense of divine love and intimacy.

Von Balthasar's concept of God's Love as the foundation of Christian mysticism aligns with the traditional understanding of the mystical path—a journey of union with God through contemplation, prayer, and surrender. His work emphasizes that the mystical encounter with God involves a profound experience of love that transcends intellectual comprehension, leading individuals into the depths of divine mystery. The true essence of our purpose can elude us when we merely navigate through the routine motions of rituals, songs, and the deciphering of biblical texts. The mystic's journey, in stark contrast, leans upon the Holy Spirit as the conduit for infusing us with the very presence of God.

Practically applying von Balthasar's insights into Christian mysticism involves cultivating a contemplative and prayerful life centered on the experience of God's Love. This involves engaging in spiritual practices such as meditation, contemplative prayer, and reflection on the Scriptures to deepen one's awareness of God's loving presence. One must be fully present with God at all times as much as one's attention can be focused.

Moreover, von Balthasar's concept of God's Love invites individuals to embody love in their interactions with others. This practical application extends beyond personal spirituality to social engagement, emphasizing the importance of compassion, forgiveness, and selfless service—a reflection of divine Love manifested in human relationships. For if God is omnipresent, we should see His Love and essence in each of our fellow humans.

Christian mysticism, influenced by von Balthasar's insights, calls individuals to live a life characterized by a deep sense of compassion, humility, and openness to the transformative power of divine Love. It encourages a radical shift in consciousness, inviting individuals to view the world through the lens of Love and grace, leading into empathy, reconciliation, and a sense of interconnectedness with all creation. Your soul should be lovingly intertwined with all that surrounds you.

Significantly, von Balthasar's concept of God's Love as the core of Christian mysticism invites believers to embrace suffering as a path to deeper spiritual transformation. This aligns with the mystical tradition's understanding of the "dark night of the soul," wherein trials and challenges become opportunities for spiritual growth, leading individuals closer to God's love and grace. Discomfort or suffering should always be viewed as a not so gentle nudging from God that there is growing and spiritual maturity that needs to occur. It is best to go through the process consciously rather than through a state of shock and extreme pain, but both ways suffice when it comes to growth and outcome. We eventually learn to handle trials and tribulations with grace and fortitude. This allows us to reflect the Love and grace that God shows us out into the world and help those who need it.

Von Balthasar's insights into God's Love in Christian mysticism also highlight the transformative power of contemplation on the mysteries of faith, such as the Incarnation and the Cross. Contemplating these divine mysteries invites individuals into a deeper understanding of God's self-revelation and sacrificial Love, fyrthering a profound spiritual union. Contemplation, meditation, and prayer are all tools to access this greater Love.

In summary, von Balthasar's concept of God as "Love," as expounded in "Love Alone," offers profound insights into Christian mysticism. This concept underscores the centrality of divine love as the driving force behind the mystical journey, inviting individuals to experience, embody, and share God's Love in practical ways. Incorporating these insights into Christian spirituality facilitates a transformative journey of union with God, rooted in contemplation, self-giving love, and a deepening awareness of the divine presence in all aspects of life. For Christians, transcending the confines of routine religious practices and doctrines to explore the depths of mysticism offers a transformative journey towards a profound connection with the divine. By venturing beyond the mundane and embracing the mystical dimensions of faith, believers can unlock untold spiritual riches, fostering a deeper communion with the sacred and unveiling profound truths that transcend the limitations of mere human understanding.

CHAPTER 7

The Rise of Rastafarianism

The Rise of Rastafarianism

Rastafarianism, a spiritual and cultural movement born in Jamaica during the early 20th century, has roots deeply embedded in Christian theology and a unique set of beliefs and practices. Its historical rise can be traced back to the socio-political conditions of Jamaica and the influence of various religious and cultural elements. The birth of Rastafarianism can be viewed as a response to the prevailing conditions, a unique amalgamation of religious, social, and cultural forces that converged to shape this vibrant movement. In the backdrop of Jamaica's historical context, characterized by a turbulent socio-political environment and the legacies of colonialism, Rastafarianism found fertile ground to take root. The movement bore witness to the struggles of a society grappling with issues of racial inequality, economic disparities, and a quest for identity and autonomy. The multifaceted influence of various religious and cultural elements, including but not limited to Afrocentrism, Marcus Garvey's Pan-Africanism, and the prophetic teachings of figures like Leonard Howell, played pivotal roles in shaping the unique tapestry of Rastafarian beliefs.

The origins of Rastafarianism can be linked to Marcus Garvey, a Jamaican activist and leader of the Pan-African movement in the 1920s. Garvey's teachings and messages of black empowerment, self-reliance, and repatriation to Africa deeply impacted the Jamaican populace, setting the stage for the emergence of Rastafarianism. He inspired large segments of populations of black people who had relatively few inspirational leaders at the time. Garvey's proclamation that "Look to Africa, for there a king shall be crowned" laid the groundwork for the Rastafarian belief in the divinity of Emperor Haile Selassie I of Ethiopia.

The figure of Haile Selassie I, formerly known as Ras Tafari, was crowned Emperor of Ethiopia in 1930. His lineage can be traced back to the Solomonic dynasty and directly to King Menelik I. His coronation was perceived by Rastafarians as the fulfillment of biblical prophecies, particularly the anointment of a messianic figure mentioned in the Book of Revelation. This event solidified the belief among early Rastafarians that Haile Selassie I was the incarnation of God, the messiah foretold by Marcus Garvey's words.

Christianity served as a significant foundation for Rastafarian beliefs, with an emphasis on the Old Testament and the prophetic texts that Rastafarians interpreted to support the divinity of Haile Selassie I. They regarded him as the fulfillment of biblical prophecies, including those referencing the Lion of Judah, citing his lineage to the biblical King

Solomon and the Queen of Sheba. Upon arriving in Jamaica for a diplomatic visit, many lined the streets and claimed to have witnessed a birthmark in the palm of his hand signaling a connection to where Jesus Christ had stakes driven into him during his crucifixion.

Rastafarianism also draws heavily from Christian traditions, incorporating elements of Ethiopian Orthodox Christianity into its practices. Ethiopia is home to some of the earliest expressions of Christianity including some of the most ancient biblical texts. However, Rastafarianism significantly diverges from conventional Christianity, particularly in its rejection of the institutionalized church and its emphasis on the divinity of Haile Selassie I. Other followers of this sect believe that Haile Selassie was a prophet and not the true messiah.

Unique to Rastafarianism is the belief in "I and I," a concept that encompasses the unity of God, humanity, and nature. "I and I" (sometimes "I n I" or "I in I") rejects the separation between individuals and emphasizes the interconnectedness of all living beings, reflecting a profound sense of unity and oneness. This concept resonates deeply with the biblical notion of God's omnipresence and the biblical proclamation that "the Kingdom of Heaven resides within." This profound notion encapsulates the belief that spiritual enlightenment, peace, and fulfillment are not external entities to be sought after but intrinsic aspects of our being. It suggests that within each individual exists the potential for divine connection, inner harmony, and a profound sense of purpose. This timeless declaration encourages introspection, inviting individuals to delve inward to discover the vast reservoirs of spirituality, wisdom, and tranquility that reside within their own hearts and minds.

Another distinctive tenet of Rastafarianism is the adherence to a natural lifestyle. This includes dietary practices, notably the consumption of Ital food, which consists of natural, unprocessed, and primarily plant-based foods. The avoidance of alcohol and other substances is also part of the lifestyle, promoting purity and health.

Rastafarian culture is characterized by distinctive attire, such as dreadlocks, which symbolize the Lion of Judah and a commitment to the natural state of being. The wearing of red, green, and gold—representing the blood, the land, and the wealth of Africa—serves as a symbol of Rastafarian identity and pride.

Music, especially reggae, stands as an indispensable cornerstone of Rastafarian expression and cultural dissemination. Reggae, as a musical genre, transcends mere entertainment; it serves as a resonating platform for conveying profound messages of justice, liberation, spirituality, and social consciousness. Its rhythmic beats and soulful melodies intertwine with lyrical narratives, weaving together powerful stories that encapsulate the essence of Rastafarian beliefs and ideologies. Among the myriad voices within reggae, iconic figures like Bob Marley, revered not just as a musician but also as a devout Rastafarian, stand out prominently. Marley's music became a venerated vessel, transmitting Rastafarian principles, values, and philosophies to audiences worldwide. His songs, laden with poetic depth and social commentary, carried resonant messages of peace, unity, and resistance against oppression, captivating the hearts and minds of listeners across continents. Through Marley's impactful lyrics and magnetic stage presence, Rastafarianism found an influential conduit, catapulting its teachings onto the global stage and spreading a deeper understanding and appreciation for the movement's core tenets among diverse audiences. The music of Bob Marley and other influential reggae artists continues to serve as an enduring legacy, not just within the realm of musical history but as an invaluable vehicle for the propagation of Rastafarian beliefs and the celebration of its cultural heritage on a global scale.

Rastafarianism, with its distinct cultural identity and profound spiritual ethos, has frequently found itself on the outskirts of mainstream acceptance, encountering marginalization, and enduring a spectrum of misunderstanding. This stance outside the conventional fold has often resulted in the movement facing discrimination and grappling with significant societal challenges. The tenets of Rastafarian beliefs, rooted in a reverence for African heritage, the rejection of oppressive systems, and the elevation of divine connection, have at times been met with skepticism and even hostility, contributing to its struggle for acknowledgment and validation within the broader society.

However, despite these adversities, Rastafarianism persists as a resilient and enduring cultural force. Its resilience lies in its ability to adapt and evolve while steadfastly holding onto its core values and principles. Throughout its evolution, the movement has remained resolute in its commitment to advocating for societal justice, promoting spiritual consciousness, and disseminating a deeper sense of cultural identity among its adherents.

The persistence of Rastafarianism amid societal challenges underscores its unwavering determination to uphold its beliefs and ideals. Rather than yielding to the pressures of external scrutiny or conforming to mainstream expectations, the movement has retained its distinctiveness and integrity, nurturing a sense of pride in its unique cultural heritage and spiritual legacy. This display of strength and steadfastness against the mainstream is very appealing to youth and those seeking to make sense of an ever-changing world seemingly devoid of tradition, morality and courage.

Amidst the struggle for recognition and the navigation of societal hurdles, Rastafarianism has shown remarkable adaptability. It has integrated aspects of its philosophy and culture into various spheres, including music, art, literature, and activism, contributing significantly to global cultural expressions while retaining its authenticity.

Rastafarians draw profound strength from the fusion of biblical teachings and their distinctive perspective on society as "Babylon." Central to Rastafarian belief is the reverence for the Bible, particularly the Old Testament, which they view as a source of spiritual guidance and liberation. The story of Exodus, wherein the Israelites escaped oppression and bondage, resonates deeply with Rastafarians, reflecting their own struggles against societal injustices and colonialism. Through the teachings of the Bible, Rastafarians find solace, inspiration, and a framework for their worldview.

Rastafarians perceive contemporary society, often referred to as Babylon, as a system of oppression, corruption, and materialism that stands in stark contrast to their spiritual values. Babylon symbolizes the forces of imperialism, elitism, crony capitalism, deception, and inequality that have historically marginalized and oppressed African peoples. By identifying societal structures as Babylon, Rastafarians reaffirm their commitment to resisting these systems and striving to overcome abuses of power just as David stood up to Goliath.

This dualistic worldview, rooted in biblical teachings and anti-establishment sentiment, empowers Rastafarians to navigate the complexities of the modern world with resilience and purpose. Through their faith, they find strength in the face of adversity, drawing upon the biblical narratives of perseverance and liberation to guide their actions and beliefs. The Rastafarian concept of Babylon serves as a powerful metaphorical lens through which they critique societal norms and advocate for a more just and harmonious world.

In addition to biblical teachings and their critique of Babylon, Rastafarians derive strength from their sense of community and cultural identity. Gathering in communal spaces such as Nyabinghi gatherings or reasoning sessions,

Rastafarians find solidarity, support, and spiritual nourishment. These gatherings serve as opportunities for collective reflection, prayer, and celebration, reinforcing their shared beliefs and commitment to transcending social problems. It is a people's movement that has been built from the ground up and has stood the test of time as a constant check to the powers that be. It is a movement filled with creativity, intuitiveness, positivity and relevance.

In contemporary times, Rastafarianism continues to be a multifaceted movement, embracing a diverse range of beliefs and practices. Some Rastafarians emphasize repatriation to Africa as a central tenet, seeking to return to their ancestral homeland as a means of fulfilling Marcus Garvey's vision of African unity and empowerment. Most Rastas however are content with living an "upful" life and creating a positive change within their community.

Overall, the historical rise of Rastafarianism can be understood within the context of socio-political conditions in Jamaica, the influence of Marcus Garvey's teachings, the coronation of Haile Selassie I, and the movement's unique blend of Christian, African, and cultural elements. Rastafarianism emerged as a distinctly Jamaican phenomenon during an era marked by the quest for black empowerment and civil rights. It stood as a powerful response to the pervasive inequities and class divisions plaguing the Caribbean nation. This movement bestowed upon the island's populace a profound sense of identity rooted in resilience, autonomy, and a resolute belief in self-determination. In transcending the confines of societal norms, it ushered in a paradigm shift that reverberated far beyond the shores of Jamaica. Rastafarianism remains a dynamic and evolving movement, characterized by its distinctive beliefs, cultural expressions, and a commitment to equal rights, unity, and spiritual upliftment. It upholds a lofty standard for individuals to embrace the virtuous path, gently persuading them with a blend of love and firmness to elevate their mindset. This encouragement aims to guide them towards a life that not only inspires but also motivates others to adhere steadfastly to principles that transcend the transient pressures of societal trends.

CHAPTER 8

Rastafarianism's Global influence

Rastafarianism's Global Influence

Rastafarianism has exerted a significant influence on global culture, leaving an indelible mark on various artistic expressions, music genres, and societal perspectives. One of the most prominent areas where Rastafarianism has made a profound impact is in music, particularly through reggae. Reggae music, with its roots in Jamaica, became a powerful vehicle for spreading Rastafarian beliefs, social commentary, and spiritual messages worldwide. Icons like Bob Marley, Peter Tosh, Burning Spear, the Wailing Souls and many other "roots and culture" artists infused their music with themes of justice, love, unity, and spirituality, resonating with audiences globally and elevating the visibility of Rastafarian culture. Their reach infiltrated the mainstream with artists like Eric Clapton, Paul Simon, Sting, UB40 and many more creating hit songs in the reggae style.

The lyrical content of reggae songs often carries Rastafarian themes, advocating for activism, equality, and spiritual consciousness. Songs like "One Love," "Redemption Song," and "Get Up, Stand Up" by Bob Marley exemplify the influence of Rastafarianism in promoting messages of unity, liberation, and resistance against oppression, resonating with diverse audiences and transcending cultural boundaries.

Reggae's ability to transcend cultural divides is remarkable. Regardless of language or background, people from all walks of life can connect with its universal themes of struggle and resilience. This universality has led to the emergence of reggae scenes in diverse corners of the globe, from Africa to Europe to Asia, each adding its own unique flavor to the genre while staying true to its roots.

As reggae has evolved over time, it has incorporated influences from various musical styles and cultures. From the early days of ska and rocksteady to the modern fusion of reggae with hip-hop, electronic, and even pop music, the genre continues to adapt and reinvent itself while retaining its core elements. This evolution has contributed to its enduring relevance and popularity on the global stage.

Reggae's impact as a powerful cultural force cannot be overstated. Beyond its role as music for entertainment, it has served as a voice for the oppressed and marginalized, inspiring social change and activism. Artists like Peter Tosh and Burning Spear used their music as a platform to challenge injustice and advocate for the rights of the downtrodden, leaving a lasting legacy that continues to inspire new generations.

Reggae has played a significant role in shaping the world's perception of Jamaica and its culture. The genre has become synonymous with the island nation, attracting tourists and expressing a sense of pride among Jamaicans worldwide. Reggae festivals and events draw enthusiasts from every corner of the globe, serving as vibrant celebrations of music, culture, and unity.

The influence of reggae extends far beyond the realm of music. Its distinctive rhythms and melodies have been sampled and incorporated into countless songs across various genres, from pop to hip-hop to electronic music. This cross-pollination of musical styles further illustrates reggae's impact on the global cultural landscape.

The visual arts have been significantly impacted by Rastafarianism, with its distinct symbols and cultural expressions serving as inspiration for artists worldwide. The vibrant colors of red, gold, and green—the colors of the Rastafarian flag—have become synonymous with Rastafarian identity and pride, often reflected in various art forms, from paintings to sculptures and fashion. These colors and symbols can be found all around the world.

Rastafarianism's influence extends beyond artistic expressions to societal perspectives, particularly in its advocacy for transcendence, equality, and the promotion of African heritage and identity. The movement's emphasis on black empowerment, repatriation to Africa, and the rejection of systems of oppression has sparked conversations and activism surrounding racial equality and cultural pride globally.

The Rastafarian movement's commitment to a natural and holistic lifestyle, including dietary practices and a connection to the land, has contributed to the growing interest in sustainable living and environmental consciousness. The movement's promotion of a natural lifestyle and reverence for nature has resonated with individuals seeking a deeper connection to the environment and a more balanced way of life.

In popular culture, Rastafarian symbols and expressions have been appropriated and commercialized, sometimes leading to misrepresentations and stereotypes. However, this increased visibility has had a profound impact on mainstream media and pop culture, permeating various aspects including fashion, art, and music trends. As these symbols find their way into the global cultural lexicon, they serve as potent reminders of Rastafarianism's enduring influence and resonance in contemporary society. Despite the challenges of misrepresentation, this widespread exposure has sparked important conversations about cultural appropriation and the significance of respecting the origins and meanings behind these symbols.

Rastafarianism's impact on global culture is also evident in the celebration of its religious and cultural festivals, such as the annual celebration of Haile Selassie I's birthday, known as "Groundation Day," and the observance of Ethiopian Orthodox Christian holidays, which have gained recognition beyond Jamaica's borders. Additionally, Rastafarianism's influence on societal perspectives includes its role in challenging conventional norms and advocating for alternative approaches to spirituality, social organization, and cultural identity. Its emphasis on communal living, self-reliance, and rejection of materialism has inspired individuals seeking alternative lifestyles and perspectives.

Despite facing marginalization and misconceptions, Rastafarianism continues to influence global culture by fostering a sense of unity, spirituality, and social consciousness. Its impact on art, music, societal perspectives, and activism has contributed to a broader cultural landscape that embraces diversity, co-equal justice, and spiritual awakening. Rastafarianism's enduring legacy lies in its ability to inspire positive change, uplift communities, and advocate for a more inclusive and compassionate world.

CHAPTER 9

The Rastafarian "WAY"

The Rastafarian "Way"

Rastafarian values are deeply rooted in principles of reasoning (seeking truth), anti-oppression, spiritual consciousness, and a natural way of life. These values serve as a catalyst for activism, advocating for change, equality, and the dismantling of oppressive systems. Opposition to oppressive systems has been a fundamental tenet of Rastafarianism since its inception. The movement emerged in response to colonialism, racial discrimination, and social inequalities prevalent in Jamaica and beyond. Rastafarians reject systems of oppression that perpetuate racial discrimination, economic exploitation, and injustice, advocating for equality, liberation, and empowerment of marginalized communities as well as individuals alike.

Central to Rastafarian activism is the belief in black empowerment and the recognition of African heritage. The movement seeks to reclaim African identity and culture, challenging the legacy of slavery and colonialism that stripped Africans of their history, culture, and dignity. Rastafarians emphasize pride in African heritage, advocating for a reconnection to African roots and a rejection of Eurocentric standards imposed by colonial powers. This speaks to the natural longing we all have for a connection to our ancestors, a cultural identity, and a need to carry on with traditions so that they cannot be lost or taken away from us. It is well noted that to forget our history condemns us to repeat the mistakes of the past.

Rastafarian activism intertwines spirituality with social consciousness and a deep respect for humanity. The movement's spiritual foundation influences its approach to standing up for what is right, emphasizing compassion, empathy, and the interconnectedness of humanity. Rastafarians perceive activism as a manifestation of their spiritual beliefs, calling for solidarity, unity, and collective action to challenge oppressive structures. This contrasts with some who seek to find escape from the world through religion or to take a very solitary introverted path. Rastas feel a profound sense of obligation to engage with the world in order to bring it back to a natural harmony and speak up when there are manifestations of destruction and corruption.

Rastafarian values advocate for a natural and holistic lifestyle. The movement promotes a connection to the land, reverence for nature, and a rejection of materialism and consumerism. Rastafarians advocate for sustainable living, embracing a natural diet known as Ital, consisting of unprocessed, whole foods. This emphasis on a natural lifestyle aligns with activism for environmental conservation, sustainability, and ecological awareness.

The rejection of materialism and consumer culture within Rastafarian values correlates with activism against exploitative economic systems. Rastafarians challenge crony capitalist structures that prioritize profit over people and advocate for economic justice, fair distribution of resources, and equitable opportunities for all. Similarly, Rastas will not hesitate to call out government corruption and overstepping. Rastafarian activism manifests through various forms, including music, art, grassroots organizing, and community initiatives. Reggae music, deeply intertwined with Rastafarianism, serves as a platform for social commentary, activism, and consciousness-raising. Icons like Bob Marley used their music as a tool for advocacy, spreading messages of love, unity, and resistance against oppression.

Rastafarian values extend far beyond individual beliefs and practices; they encompass a broader ethos of communal living and solidarity that shapes the fabric of Rastafarian communities. At the core of this philosophy lies a deep-rooted commitment to fostering interconnectedness and mutual support among members. Embracing principles of communal living, Rastafarians prioritize collective well-being over individual gain, emphasizing the importance of sharing resources, knowledge, and labor for the betterment of all. This communal way of life transcends mere cooperation; it embodies a profound sense of unity and shared purpose, binding individuals together in a tightly knit network of solidarity.

Within Rastafarian communities, mutual aid is not just a concept but a lived experience. Members actively engage in reciprocal acts of kindness and assistance, offering a helping hand to those in need without hesitation or expectation of reward. Whether it is sharing food, shelter, or emotional support, the spirit of generosity and compassion permeates every aspect of communal life. Through these acts of solidarity, Rastafarians cultivate a culture of empathy and interconnectedness that serves as a bulwark against the isolating forces of modern society.

The communal approach to activism within the Rastafarian movement amplifies its impact on societal issues. Rather than relying solely on individual efforts, Rastafarians come together to address systemic injustices and advocate for change on a collective level. Whether it is campaigning for social equality, environmental sustainability, or economic empowerment, the power of community mobilization is harnessed to effect meaningful transformation. By pooling their resources and expertise, Rastafarian communities wield a potent force for impartiality and positive change.

The emphasis on communal living within Rastafarianism not only strengthens bonds within the community but also serves as a powerful catalyst for social activism and empowerment. Through mutual aid, cooperative efforts, and a shared commitment to justice, Rastafarians embody the principles of unity, solidarity, and collective responsibility. In a world often characterized by division and individualism, the communal values of Rastafarianism offer a compelling alternative—a vision of society rooted in compassion, cooperation, and shared humanity.

Rastafarians demonstrate remarkable courage and strength in the face of adversity through their unwavering commitment to their beliefs, their resilience in the midst of persecution, and their steadfast pursuit of righting the wrongs of society. Rastafarians often face discrimination and marginalization due to their distinctive appearance, beliefs, and cultural practices. Despite this, they boldly assert their identity and faith, refusing to conform to societal norms that may compromise their spiritual integrity. This defiance requires immense courage, as it often means challenging entrenched systems of power and enduring social stigma.

Rastafarians exhibit resilience in the face of persecution. Throughout history, adherents of the faith have endured persecution, violence, and oppression, particularly in the context of colonialism and systemic racism. Despite these challenges, Rastafarians persevere, drawing strength from their faith, community, and collective struggle for liberation.

Rastafarians actively advocate for righteousness and equality, confronting injustices such as poverty, racism, and exploitation. Inspired by their spiritual beliefs and the teachings of leaders like Marcus Garvey, Rastafarians engage in activism and community organizing to challenge "bad-minded" people to promote positive reform. This activism requires courage and resilience, as it often involves risking personal safety and facing opposition from entrenched power structures.

Rastafarians demonstrate courage through their commitment to peaceful resistance and nonviolent protest. Rather than resorting to violence or aggression, Rastafarians advocate for change through dialogue, education, and grassroots organizing. This approach requires tremendous strength and discipline, as it demands patience and perseverance in the face of adversity.

Rastafarians exemplify courage and strength in myriad ways, from their steadfast commitment to their beliefs and identity, to their resilience in the face of persecution, to their advocacy for correcting societal ills and nonviolent resistance. Through their actions and example, Rastafarians inspire others to stand up against injustice and oppression, embodying the transformative power of courage and faith in the pursuit of a better world.

In addition to social and economic activism, Rastafarian values challenge oppressive systems on a spiritual level. The movement advocates for spiritual liberation, encouraging individuals to break free from mental and spiritual bondage imposed by oppressive ideologies, inviting people to embrace a deeper understanding of themselves and their connection to the divine. We are called to free our own minds from "mental slavery" which includes unconscious thinking/acting, weakness, and blind obedience to authority.

Rastafarian activism, rooted in these values, continues to influence social movements globally. Its emphasis on equality, spirituality, anti-oppression, and a natural lifestyle serves as a model for activism that addresses systemic issues, promotes fairness, and advocates for a more equitable and compassionate world. The way of the Rasta is one of creativity, strength, love, and transcendence.

CHAPTER 10

The Zen CHRISTafarian way

Synthesis – The Zen CHRISTafarian Way

Zen Buddhism, Rastafarianism, and Christianity, despite their inherent differences in doctrines and practices, stand as distinct sources of profound wisdom, each offering a wellspring of unique insights that, when brought together, have the potential to profoundly enhance and deepen the contours of a modern Christian worldview. These traditions, with their diverse philosophical underpinnings and spiritual philosophies, converge at various junctures to enrich the tapestry of human understanding. Zen Buddhism, with its emphasis on mindfulness, introspection, and the realization of the present moment, presents an invaluable perspective that fosters a deeper connection with the inner self and encourages a profound sense of inner peace and awareness. Likewise, Rastafarianism's focus on equal rights, communal harmony, reverence for nature, and bold courage unveils dimensions of compassion, environmental stewardship, strength through righteousness and collective well-being that resonate deeply with Christian ethics. Christianity, rooted in the teachings of Christ on love, forgiveness, and redemption, forms the bedrock of the Christian faith, offering a framework of spiritual guidance and moral principles that shape a believer's journey. When these diverse strands of wisdom are woven together, they create a vibrant and multifaceted mosaic of spiritual understanding, enriching the Christian perspective with a more comprehensive and rooted understanding and expression of spirituality, compassion, and the human experience. The synthesis of these diverse teachings beckons individuals to embrace a more holistic approach, integrating the wisdom of multiple traditions to cultivate a more profound sense of empathy, a deeper connection with the divine, and a more nuanced internalization of the complexities of human existence.

From the rich tradition of Zen Buddhism emerges a profound emphasis on mindfulness, urging individuals toward a heightened awareness of the present moment, and an exploration of the self that resonates deeply across spiritual landscapes. The practice of mindfulness, cultivated through Zen teachings, does not merely serve as a fleeting exercise but stands as a transformative tool, inviting individuals to embrace the entirety of their existence with undivided attention. This keen focus on the present moment, fostering an acute awareness of thoughts, sensations, and emotions, becomes a conduit for establishing a deeper connection not only with oneself but also with others and the divine.

In the context of modern Christian spirituality, the integration of Zen's mindfulness practices extends an invitation to explore prayer, contemplation, and communion with God in profoundly enriched ways. The cultivation of mindfulness aligns harmoniously with the Christian quest for spiritual depth, offering a means to attune the soul to the divine presence in the midst of the mundane. As Christians engage in prayer, the practice of being fully present opens pathways for a more profound encounter with the divine, creating an intimate connection that transcends the confines of mere words or rituals. Through mindfulness, Christian contemplation deepens, inviting individuals to immerse themselves fully in the sacred moments, allowing a deeper communion with the divine to permeate every aspect of their lives.

The incorporation of Zen's mindfulness practices into Christian spirituality does not seek to supplant Christian traditions but rather to augment and enrich them. It offers a lens through which individuals can navigate the complexities of modern life while nurturing a heightened spiritual awareness. This integration encourages a more profound exploration of the Christian faith, enabling believers to embrace the transformative power of being fully present in each moment, nurturing a deeper understanding of the divine presence amidst the ordinary occurrences of daily life. As individuals engage in the practice of mindfulness within a Christian context, they embark on a journey that nurtures a profound spirituality, embracing a vibrant and more intimate relationship with God while traversing the intricate tapestry of the human experience.

It is said by some that to sin is simply turning away from God. Mindfulness can therefore be seen as a way to constantly turn back towards God and therefore lead a less sinful life.

Rastafarianism stands as a profound advocate for humanity, equality, and a harmonious relationship with the natural world, espousing principles that echo the very core of Christian values. The movement's unwavering commitment to elevating humanity, battling against oppression, and fostering environmental consciousness resonates deeply with the Christian call for justice, compassion, and stewardship of the Earth. The alignment of these values between Rastafarianism and Christianity offers a tapestry of shared beliefs that invite an enriched Christian perspective, encouraging a deeper exploration and integration of these principles into the fabric of Christian living.

The synergy between Rastafarian principles and Christian values extends an invitation to Christians to embrace a more proactive engagement in societal issues. Rastafarianism's emphasis on human rights and equality serves as a beacon, inspiring Christians to reexamine their roles in effecting positive change within their communities and beyond. By incorporating these principles, Christians can nourish a deeper sense of empathy and advocacy for all, amplifying their efforts towards building a more just and equitable society in alignment with the teachings of Christ.

The environmental consciousness inherent in Rastafarianism serves as a poignant reminder of humanity's responsibility as stewards of the Earth. By intertwining these ecological principles with Christian perspectives, believers are encouraged to recognize the intrinsic value of environmental care as an integral aspect of Christian living. This incorporation invites Christians to revere the Earth as a sacred gift entrusted to their care, creating a deeper appreciation for ecological harmony and a more conscientious approach to environmental preservation in their daily lives.

The fusion of Rastafarian principles and Christian values offers a transformative pathway for believers. It ignites a renewed fervor for God-given human rights, equality, and environmental stewardship, propelling Christians towards a more holistic engagement with the world around them. As individuals integrate these principles into their Christian perspectives, they not only uphold the teachings of Christ but also embark on a journey that transcends ideological boundaries, creating a more compassionate, just, and ecologically conscious approach to Christian living.

Christians can glean valuable lessons from Rastafarianism in terms of standing firm, exhibiting courage, and maintaining dignity through righteousness, particularly in the face of adversity or opposition. While the theological beliefs and cultural practices of Rastafarianism may differ from mainstream Christianity, there are core principles and attitudes within Rastafarianism that Christians can find instructive and inspiring.

One key lesson Christians can learn from Rastafarians is the importance of unwavering commitment to one's beliefs and identity. Rastafarians exemplify this by boldly asserting their faith and cultural heritage, even in the face of societal pressure to conform. Similarly, Christians can draw strength from their convictions and principles, refusing to compromise their faith for the sake of societal acceptance or convenience. Christians are often persuaded to compromise their beliefs according to what may be trending in popular culture or being pushed by the levers of power in both academia and media. By standing firm in their beliefs, Christians can emulate the courage and resilience demonstrated by Rastafarians in maintaining their spiritual integrity.

Rastafarians exhibit courage through their advocacy for seeking truth and standing up for what is right. Inspired by their faith and cultural heritage, Rastafarians actively challenge oppressive systems and advocate for positive change in their communities and beyond. Christians can likewise learn from this example by actively engaging in efforts to address societal issues caused by moral confusion, emotional manipulation, and deception by those with ulterior motives. By following the example of Rastafarians in advocating for truth and righteousness, Christians can fulfill their call to be agents of transformation in the world.

Rastafarians demonstrate the importance of maintaining dignity through righteousness, even in the face of adversity or persecution. Despite facing discrimination and marginalization, Rastafarians uphold their sense of dignity and self-worth by remaining true to their principles and values. Similarly, Christians can learn from this example by responding to challenges and opposition with grace, integrity, and humility. By embodying righteousness and dignity in their actions and interactions, Christians can bear witness to the transformative power of faith and righteousness in the midst of adversity and achieve success against all odds.

At the heart of the modern Christian perspective lies the profound essence of Christianity—an ethos steeped in love, compassion, and the transformative power encapsulated within the redemptive message of Christ. The teachings of Jesus Christ, centered on boundless love, radical forgiveness, and selfless service, serve as a guiding beacon, illuminating the path toward spiritual enlightenment and ethical conduct for believers. The foundational principles espoused by Christ resonate as timeless truths, inviting individuals into a deeper exploration of spirituality and ethical living.

Christianity's emphasis on love as exemplified by Christ's teachings embodies a radical, all-encompassing love— an unwavering compassion that transcends barriers and embraces the entirety of humanity. This love extends beyond the confines of social divisions, inspiring believers to emulate Christ's profound compassion and kindness towards others, nurturing a culture of empathy, inclusivity, and understanding within Christian communities and beyond.

Forgiveness stands as a cornerstone of Christian teachings, portraying a transformative power that transcends human understanding. Christ's teachings on forgiveness serve as a catalyst for healing and reconciliation, encouraging believers to embody the virtues of forgiveness, freeing themselves and others from the burdens of resentment to be able to manifest a culture of restoration and grace.

Service, another fundamental tenet in Christianity, mirrors Christ's selfless sacrifice and humble service to humanity. Christ's call to serve others reverberates through Christian teachings, instilling a sense of duty and responsibility among believers to actively engage in acts of compassion, altruism, and selfless giving, thereby fostering a culture of benevolence and altruistic service within Christian communities. In society, we derive immense value from the exchange of services offered by individuals with diverse talents, as those with particular strengths complement and support the needs of others with corresponding weaknesses.

Christianity's emphasis on redemption and grace offers a profound message of hope and healing to individuals grappling with life's complexities and challenges. Christ's redemptive sacrifice and the unmerited grace bestowed upon humanity provide a transformative framework for spiritual growth and personal transformation. This message of redemption offers solace, renewal, and the promise of a renewed existence, empowering believers to embark on a journey of spiritual revival and personal metamorphosis.

Synthesizing insights from these traditions offers a modern Christian perspective that embraces diversity, unites the divisions in society, and evokes a deeper understanding of spirituality. The integration of Zen's mindfulness practices can enhance Christian prayer life, igniting a deeper connection to God in the present moment. Rastafarian values of individual rights and environmental consciousness can inspire Christians to actively address societal issues and care for the Earth as part of their spiritual responsibility.

The synthesis of these traditions encourages a more holistic approach to spirituality that encompasses contemplation, social engagement, and personal transformation. The meditative practices of Zen can complement Christian prayer practices, offering new avenues for spiritual growth and self-awareness. The strength and resilience in the face of social pressure that we get from Rastafarianism can encourage Christians to become a bit bolder when facing increasing displays of immorality, corruption and deceit.

The Christian emphasis on love and compassion resonates with both Zen and Rastafarian teachings. By embracing these shared values, a modern Christian perspective can prioritize empathy, kindness, and understanding in interpersonal relationships and societal interactions. The integration of these values can foster a culture of inclusivity, acceptance, and respect for diversity within Christian communities.

The integration of Zen Buddhism and Rastafarianism into modern Christian thought beckons believers towards a transformative journey—a profound shift toward a more contemplative and mindful engagement with faith. This amalgamation of traditions does not merely offer a mosaic of diverse perspectives; it extends an invitation for a deeper exploration of spiritual truths and an earnest quest for personal metamorphosis. The infusion of mindfulness practices drawn from Zen Buddhism acts as a catalyst, nurturing a heightened awareness of the divine's presence and incorporating a profound sense of inner tranquility within the Christian spiritual realm.

This enriched Christian perspective, woven with insights from Zen Buddhism and Rastafarianism, becomes a crucible for a comprehensive understanding of spirituality, social responsibility, and personal evolution. It is not just an amalgamation of teachings; it is an embrace—an embrace of mindfulness, true justice, boundless love, and unwavering compassion as indispensable components of Christian faith. It transcends the confines of traditional doctrines, igniting a more inclusive, contemplative, and purposeful Christian spirituality that resonates vibrantly in the tapestry of today's multifaceted world.

Bibliography

Books on Rastafarianism:

Cashmore, Ernest. Rastaman: The Rastafarian Movement in England. Routledge, 1979.

Chevannes, Barry. Rastafari: Roots and Ideology. Syracuse University Press, 1994.

Murrell, Nathaniel Samuel, William David Spencer, and Adrian Anthony McFarlane. Chanting Down Babylon: The Rastafari Reader. Temple University Press, 1998.

Stewart, Roderick. Rastafari: The People's Theology. Caribbean Quarterly, 1960.

Barrett, Leonard E. The Rastafarians. Beacon Press, 1997.

King, Stephen A. Reggae, Rastafari, and the Rhetoric of Social Control. University Press of Mississippi, 2002.

Smith, Noel Leo Erskine. From Garvey to Marley: Rastafari Theology. University Press of Florida, 2005.

Taylor, Ula Yvette. The Veiled Garvey: The Life and Times of Amy Jacques Garvey. The University of North Carolina Press, 2002.

White, Timothy. Catch a Fire: The Life of Bob Marley. Macmillan, 2006.

Books on Christian Mysticism:

Balthasar, Hans Urs von. Love Alone: The Way of Revelation. Ignatius Press, 1988.

Eckhart, Meister. Meister Eckhart: Selected Writings. Penguin Classics, 2009.

Julian of Norwich. Revelations of Divine Love. Penguin Classics, 1998.

Teresa of Ávila. The Interior Castle. Dover Publications, 2007.

Books on Zen Buddhism:

Suzuki, D.T. Zen and Japanese Culture. Princeton University Press, 1970.

Watts, Alan. The Way of Zen. Vintage, 1999.

Nhat Hanh, Thich. The Miracle of Mindfulness: An Introduction to the Practice of Meditation. Beacon Press, 1999.

Additional Zen Text:

Shunryu Suzuki. Zen Mind, Beginner's Mind. Shambhala Publications, 2011.

Film:

Henzell, Perry. The Harder They Come. Tuff Gong Pictures, 1972.

www.ingramcontent.com/pod-product-compliance
Lightning Source LLC
LaVergne TN
LVHW051752080426
835511LV00018B/3304